Copyright © 2020 Educate Through Nate
'WHIZZING AROUND WITH NATHAN'
ISBN: 9789887404545 (paperback)
ISBN: 9789887404552 (eBook)

All Rights Reserved. No part of this book may be reproduced or used in any manner without written permission of the copright owner except for the use of quotations in a book review.
Published in Hong Kong by Melissa Jane Lavi

Copyrighted Material

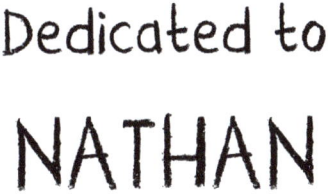

Dedicated to

NATHAN

Hello again, my name is Nate,
and a very good day to you!
It's going to be a great day.
Come along and join us too.

My good friend Nathan's dropping by.
I love it when he comes.
There's always an adventure,
and the day is filled with fun!

Just look at our cute doggies.
They go crazy when he's here.
They sit and crouch and stretch and pull,
and lick him, ear to ear.

Nathan is my BIGGEST friend,
already in his TEENS.
He tells exciting stories,
from the simplest of things.

We both love watching basketball, and
scream and shout and cheer!
And when we shoot a basket,
the whole neighbourhood can hear.

He has some disabilities.
At times he needs a chair.
I think his chair has powers,
that are magical and rare.

Maybe it's a super-chair,
with many hidden spells.
That whisk you off to other worlds,
through dusty caves and wells.

I love to ride his super-chair,
and WHIZZ and SKID and ZOOM.
We laugh out loud, it's so much fun,
as we SHOOT around the room!

But best of all, HIS STORIES,
they keep me on my toes.
And make me wonder where we'll go,
as only Nathan knows.

He loves to have adventures.
At home and all around.
OH MY GOSH, JUST LOOK AT THIS,
is he really upside down?

Once we flew together,
on a brand new airplane.
For hours and hours and hours,
he kept me entertained.

He told me of fairies and monsters,
that live up in the sky.
Of magic and mystical creatures,
in the clouds that floated by.

Whether we are on the ground,
or high up in the air,
It's always an adventure,
whenever Nathan's there.

And when the day comes to an end,
and there's not much left to do,
Nathan STILL has stories,
like the time he turned bright BLUE.

We're off to shoot some ball now.
It's been a fun filled day,
with stories and adventures,
and now it's time to play.

WHAT A GAME!

COME ON NATHAN,
IT'S YOUR TURN!

For more about Nathan,
check him out on youtube.

'I AM NATHAN: The film - Teaser'

www.ingramcontent.com/pod-product-compliance
Lightning Source LLC
LaVergne TN
LVHW070441070526
838199LV00036B/680